978-1-944393-21-2
Printed in the United States
200 lined pages
50# creme paper

Piscataqua Press
142 Fleet St.
Portsmouth, NH 03801
www.piscataquapress.com

www.ingramcontent.com/pod-product-compliance
Lightning Source LLC
Chambersburg PA
CBHW032106280326
41933CB00009B/766